Physical Mechanism
of Love

Ali Baghchehsara

Editor: Paula A. Castro
Graphic Designer: Beeke Janssen, Ramtin Jamshidi

ISBN: 9798664250848

Dedication

Warren Buffet - a famous American businessman says, "the two most important things in many cases are time and love, and you can't buy any of them."

I agree with him. My contribution thus to that is to help understand love, from a comparison to rules of physics and science.
I would say writing this book has been enriching for my journey as a person, an entrepreneur. So I dedicate this book to many entrepreneurs, and engineers who would like to help the humanity move forward.

My next company, a space company that its team is built upon on this theory mostly in terms of hiring.

If love and time are something we need, my intention with publishing the draft of this book is maybe it is urgent to for me and this book to help sooner.

Ali Baghchehsara

Acknowledgment

I like to express my deepest gratitude to those who supported me in bringing this book to reality. I also like to thank my fellow Jorgen Skatland, who has helped me to realize many things that has been incremental to me and writing of this book. He has been not only a professor with knowledge and patience but a somewhat like a psychologist who have helped me understand the universe and myself at the same time.

In many positions and situations that it felt nothing but pain, I remember one night that I was naked in my room in Norway in -27 Celsius just because I felt relief of a pain that I suffered from for 12 years. It was incredible to understand how some of my issues root back to my parents and grandparent's issues. Those may or may never leave you but active understanding of them may enable one to overcome the effects of it, such as fundamental worrying and fear.

Without the help of Jorgen, it would have been extremely difficult to go through this journey. I also would not have been able to write the information as clear as it is is in this book, without continiues support of Paula Castro, Prisca Klass and David Calvo Civera for over the last 4 years. I appreciate every single one of the Sunday meetings until we published this book for the first time, in May 2022.

Table of Content

Preface   5

Newton Physics Approach   7

1.   Thinking in Three Dimensions.   8

2.   The three Dimensions of Love   11

3.   Laws of Newton   13

1.   Perspective   19

Atomic Physics Approach   20

2.   Humans and Atoms   21

3.   Proton   21

4.   Neutron   22

5.   Electron(s)   22

6.   Need for Integrity or for Love   23

7.   Electronic Dimensions: 23

8.   What is the Heart dimension? (x)   24

9.   Same applies to Body (y) and Brain (z)   25

10.   electron (n=1) Body (y)   25

11.   electron (n=1) Brain (z)   26

12.   Heavy Nucleus Atoms   27

13.   Light Nucleus (Atom)   27

14.   Integrity / life   28

15.   Function of High Integrity   28

16.   Atomic Resonance   29

17.   Bad and Good Resonances   30

18.   How do the electron heart, electron brain, and electron body
change their original orbits?   30

19.   Although tough situations change us, but also ultimately
decisions may do. What happens then?   31

20.	What impacts it?	31
21.	How is RNA happens to project something else than what is/was?	32
22.	Stages of Life	33
23.	Function of biology	33
24.	What is the misuse of this?	34
25.	Definition of Ego:	35
26.	Selflessness:	37
27.	Selfishness/ Self-worship:	37
28.	Apathy:	37
29.	Chemistry & Attraction	37
30.	Self-Understanding & Challenges	40
31.	Chemistry modeling	42
32.	Genuine Attraction	42
33.	Myths of attraction	43
Quantum Physics Approach		45
34.	Information	46
35.	Will or un-Will / Information based	48
36.	Implacability	48
37.	Love is a decision - a very deep one	49
38.	What is a Relationship from the Quantum viewpoint?	49
39.	Falling out of love (star explosion, or simply 0 and 1)	50
40.	Preserving Love / Relationship (under-developed)	50
My Learnings		52
About the Author		54

Preface

I want you to know why I'm writing this, that's because I had an understanding, I want other people to have too. A take that helps them understand how the physics of the universe work, and the similarities between the mechanical definitions and explanations of our bodies, brains, and the universe, and how love is a part of it.

I almost feel that love is a tool that makes it possible for humans to be together and not kill each other, but it's also a beautiful story that each of us experiences in a different way. *But if we understand how it works, especially for us engineers and physicists, then we can explain love in terms of pure science, and have a better discernment of our bodies, our feelings, and emotions.*

I have been thinking for a very long time about how I can explain difficult topics to others in a way they can understand. Sometimes it can be done when you break complexity down, as it becomes much easier to grasp. It was even more interesting to explain love. That was the first question I asked all the members of the group that joined the writing committee of the book: what is love?

So - *what is love for you?*

I asked this question to every member of the team before they joined this project. I suggest you ask that question to different people - you will be surprised. As a new member of this study, let's carry on with you: *What is love?* Listen to your intuition and keep it short. No one is going to judge you.

....

....

....

....

....

....

....

If you haven't answered this yet, please write it here and keep it safe until we review the definition of love. You will get a chance to come back to it.

First Segment

Newton Physics Approach

"Classical Physics is often called Newtonian physics

because nearly the entire study builds on the work of

Isaac Newton. Newton's First Law of Motion: A body

at rest will remain at rest, and a body in motion will

remain in motion unless it is acted upon by an external

force. "

1. Thinking in Three Dimensions.

We all know that our universe is three-dimensional. That means space has width, height, and depth. With these dimensions, we can point to a certain position. Let's say you are on vacation and need to tell the people renovating your house where you want them to hang your new lamp. Even though this might never happen, you could tell the works exactly where the lamp should be placed by giving three dimensions: 0,5 meters from wall A, 1 meter from wall B, and at a height of 1.5 meters. If they follow your instructions, nothing should go wrong with it.

The dimension of an object is generally accepted as the minimum number of coordinates needed to reference a point of it. Our universe consists of 4 dimensions, 3 dimensions of space (height, length, and width, seen in a system as x, y, and z), and a dimension of time. We can tell them apart because movement in space includes various directions, while movement in time is yet to be proved to be in more than one direction.

Love can be defined in Heart (x), Brain (y), and Body(z) dimensions. The brain dimension refers to thoughts. The body dimension refers to sexual and physical attraction or the lack of it -but it goes beyond that-. And the heart dimension refers to feelings and emotions, caring or not about someone. The position in each dimension is not necessarily permanent. Things may change and the position of the body, heart, and brain may change too!

For people, love exists in the three dimensions: (i) Brain, that's where thoughts are produced, there needs to be mutual understanding and admiration between lovers. (ii) Physical, that being sex and attraction. Humans are shallow, and that's okay, when you want to be with someone it's usually because you feel a physical attraction to them. There's also love in sex. And (iii) Heart, here come the feelings, empathy, compassion, respect, having the same values. And in a dimension of time that works just in the same way as it does in our universe.

Every single person has a position in the three dimensions. Your beliefs, your consciousness, and your curiosity; your senses, your charisma, and your lust, or lack of it; your kindness, your aspirations, your doubts, and your perception of others, along with many other characteristics, put you somewhere in each plane, those are your coordinates. When someone finds a partner, a vector starts connecting them.

The bigger the magnitude, the more differences that exist between them. Having a similar position, or even positions that overlap, doesn't determine the quality of a relationship, as people are complex, and their actions and opinions are not dictated by their location in a hypothetical coordinated system. Similarly, some people can make a relationship with people on a whole different octant work, and some people don't, it depends on each person.

People can't always be found in the same coordinates they were before, they move in the three dimensions, because they age, because they learn, because they move geographically, because they get hurt, because other people make them change. That's why their relationships change magnitudes and positions.

Time affects relationships, and because humans are not eternal, love isn't either. It can last in time, but it will inevitably end because they may fall out of love, problems may become bigger than the Feeling (explained below), or something as simple and tragic as someone passing away.

People's coordinates moving and their relationships too can be a result of things as mundane as growing old, and sometimes it might be a change of geographical location - someone who is closer to you might be more attractive at a given moment. These movements are not always stable. Therefore, the movements can have a vector or record of movement. Two people who are always attracted to each other may follow each other's path, or may get bored, or simply decide to leave it at that point of the time.

This also means love can rely mostly on only one or a combination of the three above dimensions. Let's look at that from a mechanical point of view. In the following section, you'll see the dimensions depicted in a graph just like in a math or physics book. Don't get scared, we won't start deriving long formulas!

The author wants to determine how similar these concepts are and give you an instrument to help you understand what he is thinking.

2. *The three Dimensions of Love*

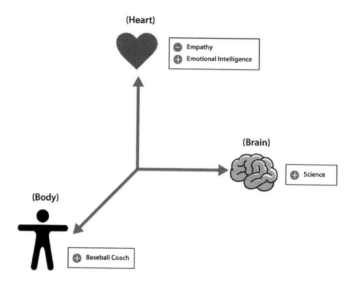

In the picture above, it is depicted that not only points are given, but a vector is created between those points -very similar to physics-. It resembles a relationship between two people.

A relationship carries love, and it has shadows, or understandings of each person. The strength, and probably base of any relationship, could be defined as an interaction of those shadows, using the general formula of Force

1. Force, or Feeling (F) -Mass or power or Momentum (M) & Acceleration or Transaction of thoughts or Attraction (A)-.

2. Transactions of experiences (e.g., thoughts in brain, touch in physical, deep talk in heart)

3. Acceleration

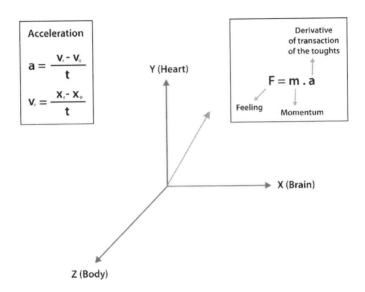

Second Law of Newton

1.   Force or Feeling (F): Mass or Power (M) times Acceleration or Attraction (A). It's the base of any relationship, it's what draws people together.

It's the product of Brain, Physical, and Heart.

2.   Power (M): each person comes with needs, desires, and preferences that affect others. Handing and taking power without breaking boundaries is important to keep the dynamics in a

relationship.

It may feel that it is mostly Brain and Heart or the body. But the person's character has a stake in this. But it is important to note that it is different for every person. (Will be explained more later)

3.   Attraction (A): Derivative of transactions of experiences or Speed (V). When being together creates a different perception of the other person.

As it is a derivative of a change in position in function of time. Here is where the 4th dimension comes in.

3.   Laws of Newton

The study of the Universe has two general approaches. Newtonian came first, the Classical Mechanics that describes the forces that act on matter, it is a simple explanation of the Structure of the Universe that for several centuries, was probably the most fundamental concept of Physics; but as it was brought to light that Quantum Mechanics -they dictate that objects have both characteristics of waves and particles- are more accurate for atomic and subatomic scale, it has been since preferred over the first outlook.

Now, not only is each person a world, but love is also unexplored, and it could very much behave like our Universe, so why not, use those approaches, to try and understand its nature. What are humans if not objects that are in constant motion? Newton's laws accurately describe the demeanor of the movement of objects, and they are not only some of the Major Laws of Physics but can spell out briefly how affection works.

First law of newton

Every object in a state of uniform motion will remain in that state of motion unless an external force acts on it.

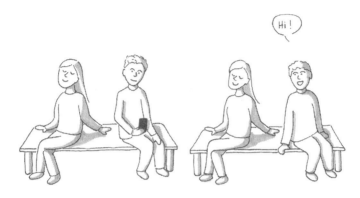

No action...   *You need action to get a reaction.*

Better known as "an object at rest will stay at rest, and an object in motion will stay in motion unless acted on by an external force." When the net force applied to an object is zero, the velocity of said object is constant (no variation). Any change in the force will affect the velocity, creating acceleration, it can be in the same direction as the movement (positive) or the opposite direction (negative).

We all have seen a picture of a still soccer ball, a foot kicking it, and then the same soccer ball moving. In life you can be the soccer ball or the foot, maybe both, but not at the same time. To engage in a relationship, you must move someone, or be moved by someone; objects at rest don't meet by themselves.

Applying a force on an object will create acceleration in the direction of the force. When people are on the same page, that's because one of them pushed lightly the other one, to keep them walking on the same road. Acting on your feelings may make someone else act on theirs.

Love can also stop you, for the better. When you are rushing, you spend so much time worrying and stressing about everything, that you forget to enjoy life. That's when a force from the opposite direction slows you down, another person can make you focus on the things that really matter, like love.

Or for the worse because when it stops you, it can drain you, keep you from growing, and from going somewhere as a couple. Know the right amount of force and direction in which it needs to be applied.

The Second law of newton

Force equals mass times acceleration.

In a scenario where someone is talking about a dreamy holiday and their significant other likes the idea of it a lot, it's like it resonates with their heart or mind and that's exactly what they are thinking or feeling.

For objects with constant mass, the acceleration is directly proportional to the force applied to them and inversely proportional to the mass. Newton's first law can actually be implied from this one. Given that F=ma, when a equals 0, F becomes 0.

If we go back to the definition of Feelings, Power, and Attraction, you can note Attraction may be affected by the balance of power, but as feelings grow, there won't be a lack of attraction.

From another angle, if you were to see a relationship as a solid box, and what you put into it as the force, you'd have to give an amount that goes accordingly to the weight of said relationship if you want the acceleration to grow, or in other words, you want the relationship to move forward. The force or feeling will grow as much as you want it and let it to.

In the same way, a more casual relationship, such as a fling, a hookup, or a holiday love, doesn't need much force, since it's not as meaningful, it will be lightweight, the box will be easier to move, and the distance it moves won't matter at the end, since it's not meant to be carried for a long time.

Newton's second law of motion has been described more in the figure above.

Third law of newton (Action, reaction)

For every action, there is an equal and opposite reaction.

Referred to as "action-reaction", if object A applies a force in object B, object B will apply a force of the same magnitude and opposite direction in object A. Both forces are simultaneous.

In a way, this law is an implication of the other two. If object B was an object at rest, and object A put it in motion, then object B would keep moving forever, thus, as object B "reacts" at the exact time object A touches it, the forces "cancel" each other out.

Here is where we talk about giving and receiving. It's not only common courtesy to treat others the way you want to be treated, but also the pillar of any healthy relationship.

If you want something out of someone you have to offer them something too, relationships are based on negotiations. You put forward yourself as a partner, and you're expecting a partner too. If you want honesty, you must be clear, speak with the truth. If you want communication, you must talk about your problems and insecurities.

In a closed system, the momentum remains constant, which in theory, means that while you're invested in a relationship, your partner will be too. Unfortunately, life doesn't work that way, and sometimes you will be disappointed. But it does teach a lesson. If you are giving more, maybe you should leave, because your forces may keep moving your partner forever; and while you can, you must try and reciprocate what your partner is giving you.

1.3.2   Perspectives

Perspective can be everything sometimes. The way we look at things in a relationship, comes from our experiences, and they determine the way we view our bond. Why are perspectives different?

The three dimensions we mentioned earlier are still relevant. The world is complicated, to understand things we need others and their perspectives on matters, happenings, and experiences.

1. *Perspective*

A conventional aquarium has 4 lateral sides, if a fish is inside the aquarium, one side will give you their frontal view, two will give you their side profile view and the final one their posterior view; unless you and someone else are standing on the same side, you will have a completely different view.

If for example, you have a misunderstanding with your friend, you will be entitled to your perception of the things that happened, while they will be sure things went according to how they remember them. Now, take in consideration the water and the crystal used in the aquarium, they distort the image, that's what other people and other circumstances can do to change your perspective.

Segment Two

Atomic Physics Approach

'Atomic physics is the field of physics that studies

atoms as an isolated system of electrons and an

atomic nucleus. It is primarily concerned with the

arrangement of electrons around the nucleus and the

processes by which these arrangements change. ...

Physics research groups are usually so classified. '' –

Wikipedia

2. *Humans and Atoms*

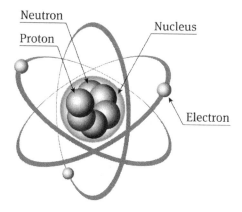

Proton = Soul

Neutron= Embodiment (physical presence, organs, etc.)

Electron= Things that makes us function, have impact (i.e. brain)

Nucleus= is our environment & home

Humans are a bit like atomic nucleus, structural and behavioral wise. The subatomic particles are the proton, neutron, and electron. Proton can be compared to the soul because the soul has a high substance and importance. Our physical presence in the world has substance too, but as it is less important, it's like a neutron. Last but not least,

projection of our DNA and experiences we've gone through causes us to have one, several or no electrons. Electrons, in fact, help us connect more with the environment.

3. *Proton*

The proton in a person is the soul, as it is the core of humans.

Many cultures and religious traditions believe the soul is our incorporeal essence. And while many philosophers discussed it being a synonym the anima (masculine: *animus*) as the animating principle of living beings; others compared it to the psyche, that reunites both the conscious and unconscious mind and creates the self.

However, it can be even more simple, your soul is just your must elemental state; what you truly recognize as yourself.

4. Neutron

If it were not for our physical form, how would we be sure of our existence?

For a while, we're permanent in this plane of reality because we are born. We experiment a lot of things thanks to our senses; our perception of the world and others, come from the mere fact that we exist.

"You are in physical existence to learn and understand your energy, translated into feelings, thoughts and emotions, causes all experience. There are no exceptions." -Jane Roberts.

5. Electron(s)

The electron is how we impact others and the environment. This applies to any dimension. The way we think, the way we use our bodies like the way we interact (like connecting through sex or physical contact), and the feelings and emotions that make us, us. Humans that not only exist and have a need to be more impactful.

6. Need for Integrity or for Love

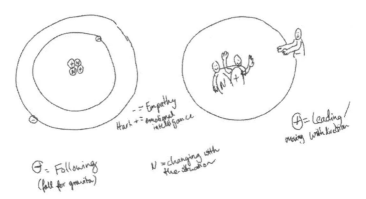

People with big souls (proton-heart), are often finding themselves in the situation of seeking Integrity. People who seek love, are more often those with big brains (proton-brains).

Rumi – famous Persian poet and scholar said "Your task is not to seek for love, but merely to seek and find all the barriers within yourself that you built against it." Also, the author believed one way to find love that is more guaranteed, is to actively go and find love within yourself, passions, things, and places you like.

However, what truly makes us able to learn, develop, and evolve into more than atoms, *smart atoms,* is the electron.

7. Electronic Dimensions:

We've already talked about dimensions, but how they are subjected by particles comes next, we're all placed in a point of a Euclidian-like space, and we're going to explore the first 3 and most important electrons dimensions or so called Atomic Orbitals in physics. The combination of our positions in all the dimensions is our essence:

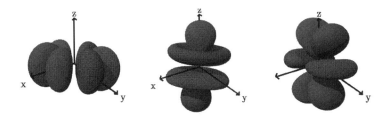

The figure above demonstrates Electron Dimensions (curated from Wikipedia).

The figure essentially means to show how Proton (quality of a person) to be in each of the following dimensions.

8. What is the Heart dimension? (x)

What you are at heart is how you feel, it also determines your behavior.

And while the soul is the core of humans, the heart is an extension to it.

An **electron (n=1) heart** is an empath, they can sense the energy and feelings in a room, the emotional intelligence comes from a faster electron, closer to the atom's core; they know how to treat others and how to deal with strong emotions.

9. Same applies to Body (y) and Brain (z)

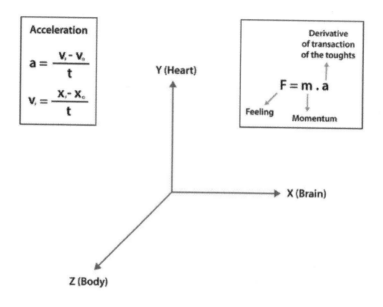

10. electron (n=1) Body (y)

It may be more complicated to discuss and understand this concept (after all, we're aware of how we act and feel, at *heart*). How you present yourself, what you do with what you're given, your talents and your abilities come in hand with your identity, how you physically treat others and even how others may perceive you. It's necessary to master one's life, the understanding of the self and what you're capable of or not, what you came with, in your initial configuration (a kid, is known to be in the most natural and untouched form, but it changes quickly as we grow up and go through experiences and understand / misunderstand things.)

The worst misunderstanding is misunderstanding your dimensions.

This also refers your abilities, and your very own self.

However, not only what we do with our bodies come here, but how our bodies react to other people and external stimuli, e.g.: attraction, libido, physical contact, sex compatibility.

An **electron (n=1) body** is great at giving away, finding ways of helping; their touch is measured, they know when to give a hug, and when to hold a hand. They are reserved when it comes to mannerisms, and it helps to drawing people close, as well as feeling deep attraction.

11. electron (n=1) Brain (z)

Deeper than the last two, it's the brain. The way you think, how you understand things and how you process information, it's highly guided by your identity.

An **electron (n=1) brain** is fast, because an electron orbits and moves around; however, it doesn't have necessarily a lot of substance. They think things thoroughly, and they express themselves in a way they can be easily understood. They can easily change environments, they adapt to new people and new groups because of how light they are.

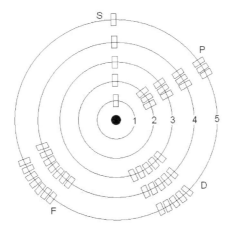

N=1 is layer one (faster electron, closer to the self), like close(r) friends

N=2 is second layer (slower electron, less close to the self),

N=3 is a third layer (even slower electron, not so closer to the self)

You know how the sun's gravity attracts the planets in the solar system? In fact, its force is what creates their orbits. Similarly, the earth attracts the moon and creates a synchronous rotation, and that's why we always see the same side of the moon, because it spins on its own axis while moving around our planet. That, on simple words.

12. Heavy Nucleus Atoms

The thing is, some people may want to be like the sun, and expect all the people in their lives to orbit around them. They believe they are the center of their social groups, or even insist on being it; some people don't even push others to create this dynamic. Their gravity is just that great.

On a smaller scale, some people may treat they relationship as if they were the earth, and their significant other the moon; someone may want their partner to follow them, only move in the direction they move, and always give them the same thing they are expecting while not giving the same.

13. Light Nucleus (Atom)

However, people who don't attract or keep people close (people who gravitate around others), may like being in this position, giving support is the preferred for some. Some people may be trapped in a relationship where they don't feel as equals, but the gravitational force from the atom (or person) near them is so strong that they can't walk away.

14. Integrity / life

Integrity is the way that your proton, electron, and neutron harmoniously work together and around each other.

The highest level of integrity is knowing who you are and the journey to become it. Maintaining it requires integrity.

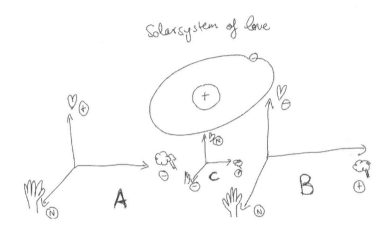

Solarsystem of love

15. Function of High Integrity

This goes along with Trust to create it and high Substance to maintain it. In other words, people with high integrity will have the control to create attraction to them by way of other people's ability. It looks like they've got something that attracts others, but it's not really them. In the naïve world of today, it may sound like someone who has worked at the White House, or Air Force, or built a million-dollar company will attract anyone.

But the truth is they had it before they built all these things around them. They understood themselves and built around their leadership skills -or that's what we like to think- to their advantage. This is like gravity, something that things with very large masses have.

16. Atomic Resonance

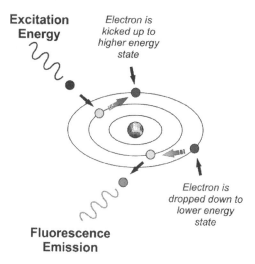

This is how people can get along together or, as they says we vibe together. Every person has a natural emission frequency that if it has been deployed and disturbed the person will be disturbed.

Two people with the exactly same emission frequency can be destructive to each other.

This is demonstrating in brain dimension how one can talk and understand someone else. The importance of communicating is meant in fact to of capturing fluorescence, and excitation emissions. So two people can align themselves.

17. Bad and Good Resonances

Bad Resonance   **Good Resonance**

Often it is said that interactivity of humans can be good or bad, and and there are frequencies between people.

In the bad (destructive) resonance example natural mode of, let's say, a suspension bridge, it's the frequency it vibrates with when it is disturbed by wind, earth movements and other phenomena and gets destroyed.

An example of a good resonance is (a good) duet of piano and violin. It can have a set of frequencies, and can produce a beautiful sound in combination.

18. How do the electron heart, electron brain, and electron body change their original orbits?

It feels like the the orbits which brain, body, and heart (electrons) are located are identical elements to a human being (DNA). However, as since birth we start developing and growing, we learn and mis-learn as our surroundings teach us stuff. Government, Television, Media,

Parenting, Fear, Anxiety and Loss of loved ones are main things that often seen to affects which orbit carries our brain, body and heart dimensions. Since we are not physical objects, or atoms, RNA(s) are what projects these 3 or more orbital distances. Fact is however that the speed of these electrons may or may not change, depending on what has affected us.

19. Although tough situations change us, but also ultimately decisions may do. What happens then?

While the identical DNA maybe is what's better, the RNA can overlearn and completely diminish multiple parts of the DNA. However, this can be good or can be bad, depending on what that is. For example, faster electrons position themselves in higher orbits and thus may feel losing self-value or self-love. In a more practical sense, it is always good to understand who one is. Changing in that direction would create a great RNA so that that person – knowing who he or she is- operates at its best in the given environment.

20. What impacts it?

- **(Context of growing) Appearances, Culture, language, communication,**
- Looks preferences (e.g., how hair color sometimes matters, how height sometimes does and how none of that will count in love),

- Gender (if you are a heterosexual woman, you will not feel attraction towards other women)
- Communication / miscommunication (effective communication between two people will make it easier for them to be attracted to each other)

21. How is RNA happens to project something else than what is/was?

Do Environment, Behavioral Characteristics and Circumstances, impact the proton, neutron, or electron state in a dimension? NO, but they will change the course of use (or misuse) of it

An example we can look at is the order people are born with respect to their siblings (if they do have siblings).

First Kid: The oldest kid is usually dependable, most of them develop a caring personality as they feel the need to look after their younger siblings, sometimes even having their parents rely on them for help, giving them responsibilities at a young age. They tend to be like Electron heart n=1.

Middle Kid: In fiction, they are often depicted as the forgotten one, when they are just the most independent: their parents are no longer first-time parents, and their younger siblings usually get the better treatment, thus making them see for themselves. They resemble Electron Heart (n=2).

Youngest Kid: The youngest kid is hardly unrestrained. As most of them grow up sheltered, being protected by their parents and their older siblings, they usually have high self-esteem that needs to be reassured.

They may often be Electron (n=3).

This is not accurate, but a commonly known myth that you may or may not be able to relate to, **just** for you to understand the concept better.

Only Child: The personality of an only child can vary. The way they are treated not only by their parents, but also other members of their family can make them self-centered, or on the contrary, considerate. They can be Protons, Neutrons or Electrons.

22. Stages of Life

It impacts and may change of orbits of the different electrons. This often will result in lacking of self-worth

Being a Proton, a Neutron or an Electron is not unalterable. Going through the different stages of life may change a person. Many kids go from being initiators to just being there, starting as positive and becoming more neutral; entering adulthood molds a person into their true self, and it could be the same person they were as kids, but sometimes it changes them into a whole "different" person.

23. Function of biology

Biological elements affect us a lot more than we think. They make us think in a certain way at different ages. However, these also come along with experiences we've gone through. Sometimes we become more cautious or less courageous to do or not do certain things.

For example, at a certain age we start to think more about copulating, biologically, it becomes more interesting.

Evolution plays a role in it as well. So, for example if a proton is in an environment where protons don't function properly, they might try to become an electron. In fact, they will become an electron or stay a proton, but they will project an electron. This in my opinion is very dangerous and might hurt the longer-term success of a person, or happiness eventually, because they wouldn't be doing what they're naturally made for, instead they'll start to act in someone else's shoes which they aren't.

24. What is the misuse of this?

In nature, protons can't become neutrons. They need to transform to become an electron or anything else. Essentially, it all starts with taking a decision and standing by it. What changes over time -in hard times- is the projection, same way DNA has its RNA and will adapt to the environment and new conditions, like the vaccine helped it to learn about COVID. It may have to learn the hard way in order to change and be compatible with the environment. Rebels and revolution leaders, in the opinion of the author, should go back to their DNA and project their real selves for ultimate integrity and ultimate authenticity.

In a process called "Beta Decay", a radioactive disintegration, the nucleus of an atom consumes excess energy and changes positive charge by one unit, without changing mass number. Humans don't tend to change their personalities or their dynamics with others unless an external stimulus (other people) obligates them to, interacting with others creates new ideas and understandings of oneself and others.

The problem with changing a proton to a neutron, or to an electron is that the fact remains the same: the origin was a proton.

So, imagine you are playing tennis with bowling balls for it instead of tennis balls. What is going to happen? The ball is not suitable for it, it is not light enough and it does take a lot more energy, you're going to injure yourself or others, and will have an unpleasant time. You can also imagine replacing a Honda Civics' wheel with a F-150 wheel and trying to drive the same way.

25. Definition of Ego:

Ego works like a rubber around a car's wheel. It is also like a rubber skin around the nucleus. It can be too thick, or thin.

It has however a function, protecting the proton (main wheel) and maintaining its' well-being, protecting the proton's axis is what helps the proton to stay always healthy and fully functional. It can be too little or too big. The best thing is to have the right amount of air for different purposes. We always hear about big ego, this is what it is like, but sometimes a big ego is necessary to go to a race. But this is not what you need to drive on the streets.

Of course, humans are not cars, we are intelligent, and evolution has done its job on our system and mechanisms. We should have the ability to adjust to our environment.

Sometimes the environment can create a cube shaped ego, that makes it impossible for people with a proton (who need to thrive) to drive

26. Selflessness:

We can compare selflessness to a wheel, while there is a tire to protect it, it also has a purpose to drive people around, take them to their destination. But if a tire is broken, no matter how hard you want it to do its job, it's not going to take you anywhere.

27. Selfishness/ Self-worship:

Ego can be your enemy, if there is an unhealthy concern with yourself, you will forget about others' needs and leave them behind, if you don't bring others along with you, one day when you can't get to your destination no one will help you.

On the other hand, if you fall into narcissism, you will forget the essence of the wheel, making the tire too big or too ostentatious will make it useless. Don't ever forget its purpose.

28. Apathy:

When there is a lack of interest on yourself or others, you fall into apathy. You do the bare minimum and that's okay, unless you have an emergency and need to go faster than usual, your wheels are not familiar with putting a real effort.

29. Chemistry & Attraction

Chemistry can be very messy, like our lives sometimes. Relating these two may give us some understanding of how nature works.

Here we are comparing each particle to a type of character, and how these relate can explain them briefly.

Proton-electron attraction: We all know the cliché "opposites attract"; it comes from Coulomb's law, that states the force between two electrically charged particles. Those with like charges repel each other and opposite charges attract each other.

People can follow the same rule. It's normal to see a couple where someone is bubbly while the other one is more reserved, or a friendship where someone has the ideas and the other one supports them.

Proton-neutron attraction: Proton and neutron compose the nuclei of an atom, they stick together due to their nuclear force, which attracts nucleons in a short range.

Initiators and leaders need an anchor to reality, while Protons can be dreamers, Neutrons will keep a cold head.

Proton-proton attraction: Protons repel each other but as stated above, the nuclear force keeps nucleons together.

Protons are prone to be together because they are of the same nature. People are comfortable in an environment they are familiar with.

Neutron-electron attraction: Although they are not exactly attracted or repelled to each other due to the lack of charge of the neutron, the magnetic moment of both the neutron and electron makes them interact; there is a very weak gravitational force in the atom that "attracts" the electrons towards the nucleus.

Neutrons and Electrons orbit in the same space due to the things they do, the places they frequent and the people they are involved with. It creates an exchange they are not searching for.

Neutron-neutron attraction: the reactive force between two neutron pairs is a repulsion. Thus, neutrons repel each other but are attracted to protons. In short, their interaction is neutral (who would've guessed?)

Neutrons don't feel discomfort or interest towards each other, but they can be together as there is harmony in their bond.

Electron-electron attraction: the combined electric fields of two electrons that approach each other creates a potential energy that grows bigger as said electrons get closer, to minimize it, they repel each other. Nonetheless, electrons can pair if the repulsion is less than the attraction to the proton nearby, gaining stability.

That means Electrons rarely feel any interest towards each other, someone who is giving will look for someone to care for. But on some occasions, they can connect in order to help or look after a third part.

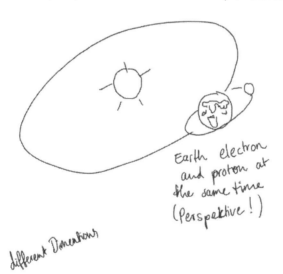

Earth electron
and proton at
the same time
(Perspektive!)

different Dimentions

30. Self-Understanding & Challenges

Start from the very beginning so you can really trust the process.

1. Try this exploration on yourself.

Make sure you read this through and understand what the author is trying to explain. Meditate the content and assimilate the meaning of each identity.

2. Observe yourself and compare how you act in contrast to others.

Take a situation you and someone else both went through, how did they react? How did you? Were you more rational (Electron Brain) or more passionate (Proton Heart)? You can also try to evaluate the relationship you have with your parents and the one your sibling has with them, or the way you interact with others and generally how your loved ones do. What is the difference?

3. Think if you understand your identity.

You have placed yourself in a point at heart, brain and body, do you really know what that says about the way you act, the way you think, the way you feel?

4. Try it with others.

Now, evaluate others, see where in each dimension you can place them, you're going to notice some of your identities overlap, or even people you share many traits with, are placed in a completely different profile.

5. Discover you were wrong about yourself.

If you go back to your own results, you may realize that you made a mistake, you're probably better suited for another identity, but you have only noticed after evaluating other people.

6. Adjust (understand yourself)

Go back to check yourself, this time, use the knowledge you acquired in the last steps, you know some identities may not be related to a trait, and you better compare them to another one.

7. Now you have adjusted your profile and basically who you are!

You can now trust your analysis, don't worry, you'll change, and your identity will too, if you don't like your results, they may vary the next time you evaluate yourself.

8. Repeat the process until you understand who you really are.

This simple theory will help you know yourself, please don't forget to focus from time to time about who you are and what makes you, you.

9. Only then you can really judge others (judge in the sense that you identify their identities)

Now, you can evaluate your family and friends, and maybe talk to them about the concepts discussed here, see if they agree with your discovery or if they see themselves as something different.

10. Acceptance.

Now, accepting things may be the hardest part. People tend to avoid facing their reality as sometimes it's easier to ignore it, there is people that simply throw away eviction notices until the bank sends an officer and takes them and their family out of their house.

Accepting things as they come, however, is also dangerous. If you just accept everything that happens and don't work towards changing them (e.g., your candidature for a PhD gets rejected because your research proposal isn't fit for the program) then you are hurting yourself.

31. Chemistry modeling

While their weights and charges are different, in essence, protons and electrons are about the same. They contribute something to a relationship, and they define people.

32. Genuine Attraction

is not love! But maybe an indication to a future love...

Attraction is a feeling that, when lived and treated naturally -in the three dimensions- will indicate a potential individual the need to explore more their relationship with someone else, and possibly find feelings of love. In other words, it comes from the initial contact and results in effort put into knowing someone.

Having said that, one must proceed with caution -and naturality- which means there are common external elements that are likely to jeopardize the essence of attraction. e.g., makeup may make someone "look different", thus making whoever feels attracted to them someone different from the person that's meant to be attracted to them, affecting the whole process.

Attention: we would like to clarify that we use the term *makeup* in the literal sense of making something up, it can be cosmetic makeup, but can also mean making up a voice, a character, etc., disguising a part of you as something it's not.

33. Myths of attraction

Attraction is in simple words creating interest in someone's mind, heart, or body. There are several reasons that may make it easy for a person to be attracted to someone.

1. Reciprocity: attraction can and will grow when the other person reciprocates your feelings and efforts. When they are interested in your conversation, when they care about your wellbeing, compliment your looks and so on.

2. Proximity (Proton Electron force): when two people spend too much time together, they learn more about each other than people who barely see each other, having the opportunity to interact creates interest and appreciation.

3. Similarity: having a lot in common creates a feeling of closeness, sharing interests, such as reading, watching movies, or playing sports,

gives people an excuse to talk more and do activities together.

4. Physical environment: the way we're raised, the place we live, the things we do, all those shapes us into the person we are, and it also creates interest in one type of person of other, if you go to school to get your PhD, you may feel attracted to people with the same educational background.

Holistic idea: how one sees Intelligence/how one sees emotion/how one sees the physical, it all creates an idea of the person who could be more fitting. Let's say the girl of your dreams is someone who fulfills your requirements, then you like the idea of her, but it doesn't mean you really like her.

Segment Three

Quantum Physics Approach

"Quantum physics is the study of matter and energy at the most fundamental level. It aims to uncover the properties and behaviors of the very building blocks of nature. While many quantum experiments examine very small objects, such as electrons and photons, quantum phenomena are all around us, acting on every scale. " – Caltech Science Exchange

As a branch of modern physics, energy and matter are described at their most elemental level: quanta, elementary particles, and quantum fields.

Quantum mechanics describes nature on a more fundamental level, in a scale of atoms and subatomic particles.

While some scientists proposed particles are tiny points of matter, others said they are little waves. The easiest way to view this theory is approaching them as both. Electrons move like waves, and they also follow indescribable paths.

Quantum physics could be seen as a device in the understanding of the universe (spoiler: the universe doesn't make sense.)

34. Information

Information is what's in the deepest level of our minds. It becomes reality and changes what we do and how we behave. Imagine an old marriage, after 30 years the wife has just changed her mind. One day her husband says the same thing he's said every day for 30 years, but for the first time she will have a different reaction.

Information at its most basic form, is data. Data that we know of and we are certain of.

In quantum physics, in an event of a collision between the two tiniest particles -as in the smallest that could ever be possible in the world-there are two types of reaction that could possibly happen. 1) both particles go away in separate ways, 2) both particles that can stick together while going away.

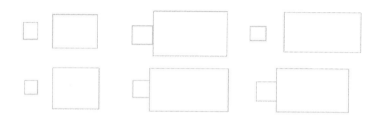

The above shows two situations where two objects hit each other. In which, the upper shows a situation where they hit and separate, and another that they hit and stick.

When the total kinetic energy of the objects remains the same, the phenomenon is called elastic collision. In a perfectly inelastic collision, the maximum amount of kinetic energy of a system is lost, thus, the objects move after the collision at the same speed, appearing to be a single object.

A collision between two people occurs when there is an exchange of information: conversations, contact, time spent together, it all gathers people together, and it can create elasticity between them (drawing them apart) or it can help them move forward. When the connection creates such elasticity that it sends them to two totally different places, then there is a change of how they perceive each other, and it can be the end of their relationship.

35. Will or un-Will / Information based

"Decision Matters" (I.e. Deciding on gender, Positive being)

Whether you think the world is the best or worst place to be in -some people tend to confuse this with feeling lucky or feeling upset due to a tragedy or difficult situation- this is irrelevant, unless that situation changes your mind, and you decide the world is now negative or positive. But being positive or negative is a decision. A decision a person can only make in their thoughts and deepest place of their mind or brain.

36. Implacability

Implacability means how much are you impacted in its most general sense. Consider a situation where you were not ready to meet anyone, but out of the blue you meet the dreamiest person in life, and you are not able to be impacted by the fact you just met them. It also may be from a strength or speed point of view. Imagine a car driving very fast in freeway and missing an exit.

In the sense this book is mainly when neutron proton or electron come close to each other but they miss to be impacted by and with each other because they are simply not impactable.

This again is broken into the brain and heart and physical aspects. For example, what makes your brain work in a different way than it usually works:

-You have great workload, and the stress doesn't give you time or energy to think about a relationship.

-You are struggling about money and finances.

(i)   Factors that impact Body:

-You are going through a difficult time regarding your health; you may be sick or recovering from an illness.

(ii)   Factors that impact Heart:

-You recently got out of a significant relationship, or a toxic one, either way you want to stay away from a romantic partner.

37. Love is a decision - a very deep one

Think about stars forming in the vast universe, they collapse due to gravity. People in a relationship, similarly, gravitate around each other.

- Love is a force, a Feeling that keeps a relationship together. Or simply brings people together.
- A relationship(s), such as friendship, marriage, kinship, is the correlation between two or more people.

Nonetheless, love and relationships are not irrelevant, we will learn this in the next section.

38. What is a Relationship from the Quantum viewpoint?

States of Feeling from acquaintances, love at first sight to spontaneous love, the point where protons and neutrons do not necessarily attract each other anymore, the start of a continuous operation. Things change, love starts turning into a relationship:

There is a turning point that transforms love into a relationship, Star Formation **(It is a decision)**

When love is about to become a relationship, it doesn't mean any part has agreed that they *are* in a relationship, that's before the elements that transform love cause the axis to join each other and become one. The proton, neutron, and electron of a person don't rotate around themselves, yet a chemical reaction nearly happens. The electron of Person A rotates around the neutron or proton of Person B, and the proton and neutron of Person A are the center of the electron of Person B.

39. Falling out of love (star explosion, or simply 0 and 1)

When love stops, we have to say goodbye, it's sad because we know it takes an incredibly huge amount of energy to go back to who we were before. We must tell our proton, electron, and neutron to rotate around ourselves. That's why we must take time for ourselves for our own sake sometimes. This is undeniably not necessary if one part is n

When love stops, or we have to say bye, it is sad, because we know that it takes an incredible amount of energy to go back to who we were before and have the proton and electron and neutron rotate around ourselves. That is why sometimes it is good to take time for ourselves. This is obviously not necessary if one was not participating, or one axis was running on idle or none.

40. Preserving Love / Relationship (under-developed)

   a) Improper creation of Error in Flirt escalation vs time OR

   b) Playing with time and flow intensity, OR

   c) corrupt quantum properties for own pleasure, OR time filing, self-entertainment, ego boost, etc. OR

d) insisting on having something from or with someone
   else when it does not exist.

My Learnings

The day I started to speak to Jorgen about this book, he kept pushing me to left or right Without giving me his opinion until I answer few questions he had, mainly around why I am writing this and why I think I have to add to the world – because he knew I have something and I did not know what that is. He also at the end of the collaboration on this book told me I am going to learn one day about the universe. It took me 2 years to do so. And I am not sure if I am right or not, but today after the journey of this book, I see the universe moving towards more integrity or dis-integrity (opposite of integrity). It does not end there; some people seek love or seek hate.

Love	Hate
Integrity	Dis-integrity

So the way I think about it now in is that we have these four categories. On the right is hate, dis-integrity and on the left is love and integrity. And people from Seeking Love and seeking integrity are moving towards each other, and people from and dis-integrity are moving towards each other. However, love may change the direction.

About the Author

Ali is an entrepreneur who has a deep understanding in Art, Physics, Engineering and has applied variety of solutions and new concepts in automotive, aerospace, cognitive science branches.

His efforts have been recognized by the Royal Aeronautical Society in (Achievement Award, London, 2014), and American Society of Mechanical Engineers (Outstanding Service Award, Montreal, 2015).

He has started 3 companies, using AI for Aerospace industry, but also started a venture capital to fund disruptive companies that generic VCs won't. He has designed the first Autonomous System for Distress Tracking in Airbus & commercial aircraft. In 2015 he influenced aerospace education with a book called "Fundamentals of Aerospace Engineering (Beginners Guide)" - no math required which became best seller on Amazon in Dec 2020.

With a Bachelor of Aerospace Engineering and Masters in Aeronautics and Management, his PhD was in the field of Cognitive Systems for aerospace engineering and Cybersecurity which he withdrew from in the last day. Presently he is building a Space Propulsion company powering space economy to be more efficient.

Made in the USA
Middletown, DE
22 October 2022

13161398R00033